The Upstairs Cat

By
Jaimi Ilama

Credits: Cover design by Laura Duffy, text by Jaimi Ilama, Illustrations by Audrey Miller, Interior design by Connie Shaw

Open Door Publishing
28531 Breckenridge Drive
Laguna Niguel, CA 92677

ISBN: 978-0-99-166521-1
Library of Congress Control Number: 2016902458

FIRST EDITION Rescue Me Series - Book One
For inquiries, contact about@anopendoor.us
www.anopendoor.us

A ton of thanks to Audrey Miller, Laura Duffy, Laura Backes, Connie Shaw, Richard J. Schwartzstein, Jess Lam, Paul and all my animals for your help, love, and support in making this book a reality. To Emily DeWaard, Alessandro Magnasco, and Estefania Trujillo for volunteering your time and understanding my passion. To Randie, Mary Ann, Lisa, and all the people who have believed in me throughout this process. Your names are etched in my heart and I am forever grateful. Finally and most appreciably, I wish to thank Max and Sam for allowing me to share a piece of their lives with the world. I love you all!

I dedicate this book to Amazon the "Real" Upstairs Cat. Watching her inspired me to write this story; a life lesson for us all. Like her, we must learn how to deal with challenges and fears. We can either face them head-on like she did, or allow them to hold us back and not move forward. Whichever decision we make will mold us into the people we become. Although change is difficult, it is also necessary.

My wish is for everyone who reads this story to be encouraged by their challenges and find their inner "Amazon".

She sits and she waits
alone in her chair,
Surrounded by silence;
her friend is not there.

Where did the boy go
who had slept in her bed?
How she misses his kisses
and pats on her head.

They both lived upstairs
in the room that they shared;
He was all that she'd known.
She is feeling quite scared.

With the room to herself,
she's feeling unsure,
Since no one is there
to make her secure.

Then she looks down the hall,
spies a boy with a grin.
And she sees a way out
of the mess that she's in.

She'd forgotten her friend
has a younger brother,
If she can't have one,
then she'll just have the other.

Though he'll never replace
the one she holds dear,
She must bravely face change.
That much is quite clear.

For so many years she was
stuck in one place,
She never took risks,
or moved from her space.

What else was she missing,
there had to be more,
Than the walls and ceilings
on the second floor.

Laugh
Love

So she gathers her strength
and musters her courage,
To brave the downstairs
and not be discouraged.

She tip-toes to the staircase,
quiet as a mouse,
And listens for noises
elsewhere in the house.

Once at the bottom,
she hears a loud sound,
As she perks up her ears
and looks all around.

In a second it passes;
speeds by with a blur,
Not sure what it was,
though she did hear it purr.

She stares at the stranger,
with eyes so wide,
As it looks back at her,
with nothing to hide.

Both black and white
with eyes of green color,
Could it be a sister
or maybe a brother?

They move past each other,
creeping so slow,
Without losing sight
of the face they now know.

Who else lives downstairs?
she wonders in awe.
A new world awaits,
who knows what's in store?

She scurries across
to a room in her sight,
Once she gets to the door,
she feels some delight.

A big bed awaits her,
both inviting and plush,
Putting all fears aside,
she jumps with no fuss.

As her eyes slowly close
in this comfortable space,
She feels a soft touch,
and starts to take chase.

"Come back," a voice calls.
"Please come here and sit down.
I am so glad you're here.
Won't you please stick around?"

She stops in her tracks
and looks over her shoulder,
To the sweet-sounding voice
that just called her over.

What was she missing
and why should she settle
When there's more to her life
than one single level?

So brave to have faced,
what was once unexplored,
And venture downstairs,
where she could be adored.

She climbs up the stairs
to the place she knows best,
Feeling proud of herself,
but in need of some rest.

At the top of the stairs,
she turns to the right.
And goes to the brother
for the rest of the night.

Love

She jumps on his bed,
and lies by his side,
Beginning to feel
what was missing inside.

Then in an instant,
she starts to play,
Watching her closely,
he has this to say:

"I am so glad you came,
I've been waiting so long."
As he pats her head,
she lets out a big yawn.

To the left of the bed,
she sees her big chair,
Now in her new room
with someone who cares.

Going over her day,
and all that she viewed,
She starts to reflect,
feeling somewhat renewed.

Purring and stretching,
she starts to recall,
A bunch of suitcases
he packed in the fall.

She remembers his clothes
scattered all through the room,
And thinks to herself,
There is no need for gloom.

OLD TOYS
DONATE
TRAVEL
DONATE

Books

Though little boys grow,
there's no reason to stress,
Whether upstairs or down,
she'll be loved by the rest.

She now understands
in the home where she lives,
No staircase can divide
all the love each one gives.

The End

WHAT WOULD YOU DO?

Have you ever felt like the Upstairs Cat?

Have you ever tried something new even if it makes you scared? If so, what was it?

Would you try to make new friends if your old friends moved away?

If someone leaves your home for a while, do you think they love you any less?

RESCUE ME

I sit here and wait for someone to come,

A face to lick, a place to run.

Someone to hold me as I grow,

And care years from now when I start moving slow.

A forever home is my wish and prayer,

A family to love me and always be there.

I dream of a home that's filled with toys,

While hearing laughter of girls and boys.

I'll give you my heart, and all I can be,

It's a lifetime of love when you Rescue Me!

38918518R00033

Made in the USA
San Bernardino, CA
15 September 2016